Roots

M.J. FARRELL

Presentation by *BookLeaf Publishing*

Web: www.bookleafpub.com

E-mail: info@bookleafpub.com

ISBN: 978-93-95784-26-9

First edition 2022

DEDICATION

This book is dedicated to the lover of my soul, who has been with me through every trial and joy. Thank you for never giving up on me and showing me how to embrace life and myself again.

This collection is for all the horizon chasers, deep thinkers and dreamers. Keep living with your heart on your sleeve.

PREFACE

This collection of poetry was written on an adventure of self discovery through truck rides with strangers, living out of a conspicuous van, and saying yes to every cup of tea and adventure on hand. It has had its pages scribbled on napkins, been flown across continents and seen its redrafting and editing on tropic beaches, under historic architecture and on dashboards.

I hope this collection of poetry encourages you to embrace your life whole heartedly, live unabashed and unapologetically, and find magic in your ordinary.

How far will they reach

What makes you?
What binds you?
What sustains you?

Questions
That centre us
Ground us

Answers
General
Or revealing

Faith in something true.
Hope in good and unspoken dreams.
Love in and from others.

But these roots
At your core,
Are only as strong as how deep you let them
grow

So do not tell me
You have love

     Act it

Do not tell me
You have hope

     Shine it

Do not tell me
You have faith

     Live it

Let your actions
Speak,
And your roots will show

Silent martyr

She feels as if she is useless

She carries guilt
For all the pain
Within humanity

She looks on her children
And blames herself for
Their shortcomings,
As if her loving heart
Was not enough

She copies what she learned from her mother, the
matron

The need to over cater
The need to be responsible
The need to help everyone but herself

But she herself sits at the foot of her mother,
A woman destroyed and broken
From a once destructive marriage,
Ignored and damaged,
The matron now fights cancer

She sits at the matron's feet

Holds her cold hands and smiles,

The matron may be withered
But in the presence of her daughter, she is truly happy

No tears are shed for the matron by the daughter,
Despite the lost relationship that her own child
mourns,
But acts in joy, patience and compassion
Encouraging her mother to enjoy life
And sing to any tune that comes by

The daughter gives this love to all she meets

Never holding back compassion
Even when taken advantage of
By children, father, siblings, lover, employers and
strangers

On the day of the matron's passing
The daughter will return again
To sit at her mother's feet and strangely
Feel warmth in her hand
And a look of true peace that has long been deserved

Oh daughter enjoy peace while living, let no-one stop
you

Thalassophile

Where are you
One who is like me
The lover of all shades of blue
The ocean and the sea

We need to find each other
Not needing a word
Telepathic with one another
Our voices need not be heard

Come, greet me
I beg, stop my lonely longing
Do answer my plea
Revel with me in the oceans roaring

You haunt me through the breeze
Your salt tang lingering
Your soul is calling to me
In every bird and bells' tinkling

I hope you are keeping well
And that you are happy
I pray you don't go through my hell
Don't get trapped like me

I'll be here
Ready to heal over tea
To adventure everywhere
As the Osprey; finally, fully free

Whoever you are
God, plant, cat or being
I'll sing to you from afar
Kindred spirit, I'll be waiting

Pigweed

Bright, deep crimson
Flows from your lips
Your generosity giving
Life and satisfaction
To all those around you

Yet this is how they thank you
With a name that brings mockery

Not only do they view you as
A nuisance
A weed which is better uprooted and destroyed
But that your bright, brilliant, benevolent love
Is only good enough for swine

But that won't stop them from using you
Getting their benefit still

You should be called Persephone
Surely that's why you only come out so often
Hades probably treats you with respect
Like the immortal, unfading beauty
You are

Please be strong enough not to need humanities
praise
Mankind is disappointing

Earthworm

I feel I have been here forever

A worm in a vast jungle
Of hot green moss
Towering canopies
Living vines
And speckled rotting leaves

The air wafts
With thick earthy notes
Humid rain and rainbow feathered flocks
The roots vibrate beneath me
Stretching and extending slowly

Varying discordant screeching
Somehow make perfect harmony
As an unseen rumbling plays the base line
Of this melody.
The same melody since the beginning.

How long has it been
Am I as ancient as these roots
Or these leaves of infinite size
Which only allows a smattering of sunlight
To reach the forest floor

But I don't recall these creatures
Roaming,
So alien are these fossils, of which
I slime over and burrow in
As if I am but a micro-organism

Perhaps I am but seconds old

Skye

Cast me off in the highest blues
I wish to fall up forever
To race, wade and float for eternity
As gravity and surface are far from my reach

I've always had an affinity to here.
This desires origin I do not know
Perhaps a hearts longing
From a time before my first breath

Why then, must I be haunted
By the looming,
Fast approaching
Dark, muddy pit

Why must my feet plant into that soil
When all my soul wants
All my soul needs
Is the chill airy embrace and kiss of heat

Instead, I am forced to
Dwell here for but seconds
And spend tortured years
In wet, dank, suffocating spaces

Surely one day
This will be my eternal fate
Thrill, freedom and awe
Are my true peace and resting place

One day I will float up again
Rush into this embrace
For even its fleeting seconds
Smears joy upon my face

Dimension

Cracked, brittled, dry wood
Offers glimpses outside our world
Of cockles and mussles
Gravity defying forests
And mermaid tails

Soft, firm, sandy banks
Seem more inviting
Than the rickety boards
That, like a pedestal,
Hold strange gods a-high

Fougerite rising around
The forced, foreign
Man-made structure
Disturbing and penetrating
The transparent surface

Gifts of betrayal linger in the sky, like kites
Calling to the babes of the tides
The children are ripped from
The wet, warm embrace
Left gasping and screaming as blood drains from
their lips

If young
The lanky beings have pity
And toss the child back
Tramatised, but alive
No wonder we are taught to hide

Yet this is natural
And the strange being's bodies
Falling off metal whales
Become our feed
No worry of whose son or daughter they were

We scaly creatures pity them
Sometimes imagine their back story
But some find it easier to ignore and simply do
Mindless and thoughtless
Of the world apart from us

Brave voyagers
That breathe on borrowed air
Take journals to document what they experience
But their knowledge is but a sentence
In the book of this culture

The strange being's from the dry
Are piteous further away from the surface
And despite our defences and air that drowns
them
They still adventure here
They did not learn that curiosity killed the
catfish

Such magic and danger
In our parallel worlds
That meet with firey kisses
As the sun and moon
Pass through the horizontal barrier

We shall stay here
And live alongside the gentle beings
The ones that float down
And take joy from our mystery
But be cautious

Fleshy creatures can not always be trusted

Lost

It is saddening
That tradition is so small

That there is break in my being.
That without food, I'd know nothing at all

Don't get me wrong, I'm glad at least this
remains
But the loss of my grandmother, and that
connection to heritage leaves me to grieve

The sauce of svíčková, plnena paprika and
stewed apples pumps through my veins
I can't help that Christmas is not real, unless
celebrated on the Eve

I can't change that Easter calls for eggs of colour
and pattern
And mazanec with lashings of butter

But on the other side I am drawn to drink
without number at pubs and taverns
Longing to eat stew dipped soda bread and
dream to roll down those hills of emerald colour

My sunburnt home, I love your heat
And that you give beauty and opportunity to an
eight part mutt

But your war fears forced roots to be abandoned,
we are incomplete
Renouncing cultures, names and language for
what?

How I wish to sing in any of my tongues
That are forever lost to me

What emptiness will their air remove when
filling my lungs
I wish my body would immediately adapt and
evolve when these places I finally see

Tamed

Perched on a golden swing
She sings
Reminiscing a day
Or dream
When gapped walls
Did not enclose around
Her small frame,
Giving her a world
With no space
To stretch her wings

It's as if this fiend
Once thought friend
Does not comprehend
That though she is so small
Is not some pet
That can be broken.
She is an eagle
With falcon claws and precision
A wing span that blocks the sun
And a voice that speaks for the wild

Oceans can not impede her flight
She laughs in the face
Of dangerous heights
Your small world is too confining
And beige.
Give her back to the burning, burgandy deserts
Moss woods, and frosted peaks,
To wind swept blades of the open plains
And salt spray off broken cliffs.
She never asked to be tamed

Pele

She is the volcanic spirit
Molten so excessive
She creates her own light and shade
Exhibiting the rare beauty of her smile

Fire breathing
Her laughter ignites
Encircling and captivating all within
Her incandescent realm

People admire her joy
Comment and visit her in her glory
Boast of her bubbling melody
Pretending that they are kindred with she

But if her passion erupts
As she roars and fights
For her rights and for justice
Her admirers flee

They find danger and fury
As she makes sense of her world
Frustrated with fair-weather friends
Expelling the ash of the friendships demise

But time will heal over
Like a wrinkled, blemished scab
And she will give generously
To be abused once again

Atlas

I want to be the type of person
Who can open an atlas
Spin around blindfolded
Playing pin the tail on the donkey
And go wherever my fingers land

To run away and explore the world
Being authentic with my fated travel-fellows
And deemed as a charismatic bonus on their
own journey

I wish to taste the spices of unknown dishes
To smell the sweat of alien animals in the wild
To burn the sight of deserts in my eyes
To feel the hands of the generous elders
Sharing their wisdom and traditions to an
outsider

I wish to walk the back streets like the
inhabitants
And drink the locals under the table
Let me dance with strangers, barefoot in barley
fields

My heart is wanting
My body is willing
My soul is needing
So brain and logic, get on side
Stop being a shell of who you long to be

Learn (and give it time)

He steps out today
Full of regret
Ashamed of the things
He cannot forget

He looks in the mirror
And can only see
The blemish
Of his indecency

His hair carries his tension
And falls to his hands
Grappling the comprehension
As the chaos expands

Fighting for normality
Instead of facing the facts
He first denies reality
Or gives up and relapse

One day soon
Light will dawn
He'll step fresh from his cocoon
The pain will be gone

He will love life again
After living penitential
Matured and humbled, a time will come when,
The shame is nothing more than inconsequential

Libérer Versailles

Timid Tiptoeing
In these halls of antiquity
Lace trimmings dipped in gold
Catches fire in the golden hour
And lights laughter
Caught in the tender twinkle of chandeliers

Inawed and out of place
Scuffed trainers squeak
On polished parquetry
That carries the clip of ancient
Handstitched heels
In the ghost of its memories

Plebeian admiration
Of the vibrant art and blood
Of history
Haunt and give light
As wealth beyond comprehension
Sparkles with generous delight

To imagine the horror
On the artiocrats faces
As commoners walk
In the shadow of their places
But their caricatures already sliced
A grim defacing

Manicured gardens
Of green and tamed wild
Reflect back through
Mirrored halls
Echoing through windows
The soul

Guilded luxury
In every step
A sight to behold
Where no-one is kept
From revelling
Anymore

Loved

Natures are strange things
Even more so when one has many
Like a chameleon changing its tone
Reflecting their emotional state

That's what you are like
But you do so and feel shame
As if the authenticity of your heart
makes you worthy to be unloved

We mourn, as we hear that you do not believe
That your worth is of the highest quality

You sit around dogs and treat them as kings
And give up your world aged just twenty
Amongst others, you are not your own
Covering your chameleon skin with patterns of
self-hate

Your mind keeps looking to strike
Landing on yourself for reasons to inflict blame
So listen to us who say you can restart
And know that you are always loved

So keep wearing your heart on your sleeve
You owe no-one an apology

Tasting

Liquid gold
Coats the wafer thin glass
Gliding down the walls
As melted butter
Champagne bubbles dance
Flirting and inviting the admirers glance

Deep oak
And summer fruits
Fill the olfactory hub
Seducing the lips
To give in and feel
The cold tang on the tongue

Zest bites the front
Smoothing the rough buds
His eyes catch sparkle
Lips forming an inverted arch
His being filled with warmth
As the elixer goes down

Power

How phenomenal is language
That it allows us to articulate
Magic, awe and hate

That it has life and character
Modality and tone
That is gives the capacity to make all things
known

What would I give to know it all
In every tongue
To know how to get each lyric strung

That I could express my heart
Through the metaphorical gaze
See every conversation in ballet

Because our voices reveal art
It's symbolic, spirited and sly
It's punny with meanings altered from spellings;
like dye

Language reveals a heart
And a human's core
Gives them the opportunity for more

Language isn't just something you're born with
It is a gift and it is power
The more you know, the less you'll cower

And the more you'll appreciate
The beauty of a flower

Highbeams

Red glowing embers hover
Fortune tellers
Of the seconds before on the tar

Each swerve we mimic
Avoiding potholes
Gracious for the Gypsie's guidance

Unique guiders with their own destination
Some are faithful riders,
Others need to learn what indicators are for

Blinding white,
Not at the end of death's tunnel,
From opposite directions sit at a stand still

No mocking though,
As we've been there before
If the opportunity arises, we suggest to take the
road less traveled

Don't lie in wait for long
Take the opportunity that's more fun
Sing with your guilty pleasure artists

You'll find landscapes and sunsets
That people won't believe are real
And feel the vastness of Abraham's decendancy
numbered above you

You'll meet hospitality
A laid back urgency to live in the moment
And the world's best pies that don't need to be
advertised

But you can stay
Stuck still and blinded
Some prefer to view bumpers

Sonnet

Born to a world of high expectations,
Never allowed to test reality,
We're given nothing but our relations
Those, which raise us as a formality

Our world view changed, when we were away
And for enlightenment we're put to shame
The older men scoff, "tis only child's play"
And their disappointment breaks our brave
frame

We have returned, and followed the custom
Breaking our children, growing them too soon
And when they return, in fragile blossom
Full of fantastic knowledge we impugn

And the circle of light dwindles once more
The young cry out for life, we shut the door.

Alarm

Is there a greater joy
Than to be woken up
By the sound of light paws
That turn into chaos
As the owners soar from the ground
Crush your stomach
And stick their loving
Wet, padded nose into your face

Eager, uncoordinated tongues
Wash your face
And your smile won't be replaced for hours.
What heart these creatures have, who have not
known you
For more than a few hours
Yet share their soft ears to your conversation
And wag their joy-ometer at a speed
Which would get a ticket on the highway

It is no wonder
That their lives are so short
As they live authentically
From the minute they are born
They have no need to make amends
No need to repent
They love unapologetically
They are purer than this world can handle

Please know this

You are stardust
The fragmented and innumerous remnants
Of an everlasting
Burning flame

You fill the universe with every breath.
Your kind reach never
Ceasing
And overwhelming

Reflecting light
You shimmer with cosmic mint
Comet hues and
Un-name-able purples, pinks and blues

You fill all empty, lonely spaces
You're the companion for the wanderer in their
solus.
You are a coruscating constellation
Leading and guiding the way

You explode
With justice and truth
And embrace those who fall
Encouraging them to their potential

You're mind is desirable
Unending
Witty and gracious
An unmissable supernova

You are the neccessary
Piece of the celestial puzzle
Without you
Nothing can sparkle

You have me forever
I'm never out of your reach
The universe is but small
And you and I have eternity

Guitar strings

Some people imagine this place
As a giant tree
Stretching out into the sky
Reaching to far edges.
Underneath everything is connected
Vines, seeds and branches
Sinking and resprouting
Creating the entire Earth

But it is also a spiderweb
Linked and held together by one cord
The silver droplet
Sends vibrations along the chain
But when half is swatted
The web is destroyed.
The trauma and devastation on one side of our home
Impacts us all

We are held together
Like one body
We are an
Unstructured melody
So raise your resonance to the bridge
As our strings are strummed poetically
Let us be tethered
And return to our united beginning.

ACKNOWLEDGEMENT

It's been a long time since I last wrote an overarching list of gratitude and I hope this small record begins to pay the debt of thanks I owe.

Firstly, I wish to thank my life givers, Jennifer and Sean, for raising me to love first and fully, I will never be able to express how greatful I am, especially to you mum, in modelling how to be a woman that honours God in every action and I hope I make you proud. Of course I also thank my sisters Dallas and Claire, and my brilliant brother-in-law Matthew Welch. All five of you have been forced to listen to my ramblings, given me critiques on my writing and have loved and supported me during the hardest season of my life. Thank you for all of your love.

I also wish to thank a few friends:
To Amy Buckley, I can never begin to express my gratitude for teaching me to embrace adventure again and live life to the full, you will never know how formative to my being you are.
To Leija Harman, Cammy Jansz, Katie Morris and Tara Komaromy, what a pleasure and joy it has been travelling the highs and lows of life with you. Your professionalism, encouragement, dedication and compassion has nurtured my practice immensely.

I am grateful to the team at BookLeaf Publishing and their #TheWriteAngle challenge for giving me the opportunity and space to beautifully present this piece, when I felt completely out of my depth. You have done a marvellous job.

I must honour my inspirations in life and writing, from writers like C.S. Lewis, Jane Austen, William Blake and Chimamanda Ngozi Adichie, to teachers who saw value in my mind when I saw none, like Luke Matthews and Angela Eynaud. To my students who believed in me at a time when they didn't know how much I was struggling, each of you are so unique and special and I hope my time with you has been as edifying as I have found your time with me has been. I can't wait to see how you change the world. My deepest admiration goes to the woman who everyone should have as their guide, mentor and life coach, Helen Toon, who is everything I aspire to be as a woman, teacher and friend. I can't imagine my life without you.

I also thank everyone who opened their drive ways, houses and lives to me and my travel buddies on the first stop of the rest of my life. Your hospitality and openness has been a breath of fresh air and influential to my core.

Lastly, and most importantly, my standing ovation goes to my confidant, inspiration and best friend, Sophie Wentzel-Lewis. You, my beautiful, loving, creative and brave woman have been with me throughout every heartbreak and joy. Your editing prowess has been of the greatest value and your wisdom and kindness has saved me from destruction. I'll do my very best to uphold you in the same manner, I'll also try not to pull you infront of a tram again.